12 walks around Perthshire

EXPERIENCE BIG TREE COUNTRY

VOLUME 1

Felicity Martin

Catkin
Press

INTRODUCTION

This guide is the first in a new series designed to bring together the best walks around Perthshire. It contains 12 routes of varying grades, ranging from 3 to 10 miles long.

As well as clear directions, each walk includes information to help readers connect with the natural world. Experience the wonders of Big Tree Country, by following the routes in this guide to places with soaring trees, the scent of bluebells, and the sound of thundering waterfalls.

The walks range from gentle strolls beside Loch Leven and the Tay estuary to hill climbs in the Ochils and up Perthshire's highest mountain, Ben Lawers. In between are moderate walks that explore rivers, woods and rolling farmland. They have been chosen for their splendid views, rich wildlife and intriguing history.

Big Tree Country – in all its fascinating aspects – is the common theme. The routes not only visit individual heritage trees, ancient woodland and newly planted native woods, but also take in rivers, follies, gardens, and even a distillery.

A car is not needed to make use of the guide, as most of the start points are well served by public transport. The majority of walks can easily be reached by bus and some are also near railway stations. Or why not use a bike and do even more for your fitness?

COVER: *River Garry (Walk 10)*
TITLE PAGES: *Perth Bridges (Walk 9)*
ABOVE: *Ben Lawers, high point of Perthshire (Walk 12)*

Walking in Perthshire

Perthshire has a greater variety of landscapes than anywhere else in Scotland and it offers a remarkably wide choice of beautiful walks.

This guide explores scenery ranging from farmland to moorland, wood to mountain, and riverside to loch shore. The walks span the length and breadth of Perth and Kinross, the administrative area that covers most of the old counties of Perthshire and Kinross-shire. Today, the whole area is often referred to as 'Perthshire' and that is the name used here.

The southern part of the area has a Lowland landscape, with wide, fertile valleys and lush coastal plains, including the Carse of Gowrie, the location of **walk 4: *Errol and Port Allen***. However, it is not all flat, as there are several ranges of rounded, grassy hills. The largest of these, the Ochils, are the some 30 miles (48km) long by 10 miles (16km) wide, and have – like the others – a volcanic origin. **Walk 11: *Glensherup Circuit*** runs along an Ochils ridge with superb views of Glen Devon and the Forth Valley.

North of Crieff, Dunkeld and Blairgowrie, which all lie close to the Highland Boundary Fault, the landscape is much more rugged in nature. Rivers and long lochs wind through deep, steep-sided glens that are hemmed in by heather-covered mountains. For a real flavour of all these elements, try **walk 10: *Loch Faskally Circuit***. Waterfalls tumbling down the wooded hillsides are another feature of Highland Perthshire, and **walk 5: *Birks of Aberfeldy and Dunskaig*** visits one of the best. Or, for magnificent views of both Highland and Lowland scenery, try **walk 8: *Knock of Crieff and the Hosh.***

Perthshire has an abundance of wildlife and these 12 walks visit some particularly rich habitats. **Walk 3: *Loch Leven and Kinross*** runs through a National Nature Reserve famous for its birdlife. Routes through woods are good for sighting roe deer, red squirrels, great spotted woodpeckers and smaller birds, such as long-tailed tits. The riverside walks offer a chance of spotting osprey, dipper and goldeneye, as well as leaping salmon and perhaps even an otter. For red deer and moorland birds, such as hen harrier, grouse and meadow pipit, you need to head for the hills.

Wildflowers can be seen through many months. Enjoy carpets of snowdrops on **walk 2: *Water of Ruchill*** in February and of bluebells on **walk 1: *Bluebell Wood*** in May, or tackle **walk 12: *Ben Lawers*** in July to see rare plants, such as alpine gentian and mountain sandwort.

The more you open your senses and tune in to the natural world you are walking through, the more rewarding you will find these walks.

ABOVE: *River Earn and Comrie White Church (Walk 2)*
BELOW: *Looking down on Crieff (Walk 8)*

Experience Big Tree Country

It's Perthshire's trees and woods that make the area so distinctive and create such an attractive environment for walking. Wherever you look, they enhance the views of river, loch, meadow and mountain.

Trees grow very well in the local climate and soils – often reaching record-breaking proportions. And for generations they have been valued and nurtured, ensuring that Perthshire now has some of the finest woods and specimen trees in Britain.

Scotland's native species, such as oak, ash, birch, rowan and Scots pine thrive in Perthshire. A good selection of them can be seen on **walk 9: *Kinnoull Hill and Perth Riverside***. The route also visits the Jim Aitken Arboretum, where an old collection of exotic trees, such as redwoods,

is being revived with new plantings of trees and shrubs especially suited to gardens.

Introduced species have found a special home in Perthshire. Local landowners became particularly keen on planting trees just as the New World was being opened up by exploration. Hearing that specimens of enormous size were being discovered in North America, they sponsored tree-hunting expeditions, keen to acquire them for their own policy woodlands.

The 'Planting' Dukes of Atholl were leaders in demonstrating the commercial and landscape value of new species. During the 18th and 19th centuries, they planted some 27 million trees on their estates, particularly European and Japanese larch, and a vigorous new hybrid – the Dunkeld larch – that arose as a result of bringing these two together.

Walk 7: *Woodend and Banvie Burn* goes through some of Atholl Estates' fine larch woodland and passes Diana's Grove, an arboretum of soaring trees in the grounds of Blair Castle. These living giants are mainly North American conifers discovered by Perthshire plant hunters Archibald Menzies and David Douglas.

One tree – the Douglas fir – commemorates both men. Its English name honours David Douglas, who sent back the first specimens, but its Latin name Pseudotsuga menziesii, recognises that it was Archibald Menzies who first identified it.

Walk 6: *Birnam Oak and the Hermitage* visits a grove of magnificent Douglas fir and passes one that vies for the title of the tallest tree in Britain – the Hermitage Douglas. It is a mere youngster, only about 150 years old, compared to the Birnam Oak, which has stood on the banks of the River Tay for hundreds of years and is reputed to be a surviving remnant of Birnam Wood, immortalised by Shakespeare in 'Macbeth'.

The Birnam Oak, the Hermitage Douglas, Diana's Grove and the Birks of Aberfeldy are recognised as Heritage Trees of Scotland, being among

the country's most remarkable and significant trees.

Walking is the ideal way to appreciate this natural heritage. By wandering through woods and getting close to trees, you can absorb their atmosphere and character.

The **Perthshire Big Tree Country Heritage and Access Project** is continuing the tradition of caring for this special environment. Phase one of the project improved access and interpretation at over 20 woodland sites throughout Perthshire. On these walks, you will use paths and see interpretation boards, wood and rock carvings resulting from this work, and also pass through woodlands now more sensitively maintained and improved.

The second phase of the project is giving attention to further notable trees and sites, including Perthshire Redwoods and the Carse of Gowrie historic orchards. Several organisations contribute to the project, which is led by Perth and Kinross Countryside Trust.

Perth and Kinross Countryside Trust was established in 1997 and aims to provide and promote high quality opportunities for access and recreation throughout Perth and Kinross.

OPPOSITE: *A Noble fir at Diana's Grove, Blair Castle (Walk 7)*

ABOVE: *The Queen's View over Loch Tummel towards Schiehallion*

1

Perthshire's ancient oakwoods have brilliant displays of bluebells and other wildflowers. Darroch Wood near Blairgowrie is absolutely stunning in spring, though the easy walk to it is popular year-round.

Bluebell Wood

Start	Blairgowrie – Whiteloch Avenue, Carsie **NO173426**
Distance	4.8km (3 miles)
Grade	■ ☐ ☐ ☐ ☐
Time	1.5 hours
Terrain	Farmland, woodland and small lochs; surfaced and earth paths

Getting there: Whiteloch Avenue is on the south side of Blairgowrie, off the A93 Perth Road. Park considerately on the street if arriving by car.

Public transport: Bus stop at the end of Whiteloch Avenue; regular services include the no. 58 from Perth.

This route passes between White Loch and Fingask Loch, both popular places for anglers and bird watchers – if lucky you could see an osprey fishing for trout.

1 **NO173426** Walk away from the main road along Whiteloch Avenue to the end and turn right beyond the houses onto a tarmac lane. Follow it across farmland to White Loch, which is used by the local angling association. This is a good place to see coots, grebes, ducks, geese and swans. Just beyond the jetty, take a path to the right over a bridge across the outflow of the loch.

2 **NO167429** Follow the north shore then cross stepping-stones into Druidsmere Wood. The path runs along the left side of a fence enclosing woodland. Stay beside the fence, forking right under oak trees, to reach the main road.

3 **NO173431** Turn left along the A93. Opposite Golf Course Road, fork left through bollards. Cross Ardblair Road and keep ahead up Ardblair Terrace. The lane bends left by a play area. Continue ahead on a path beyond the houses. It leads up the left side of Ardblair Wood, an ancient woodland.

4 **NO169438** An information board about Muirton of Ardblair marks a junction where the route turns left into this small settlement. Walk past the first buildings then, just before a farm, turn right through a gate on to a fenced path that skirts the farm. Bear right at a field corner on a hedgerow path up to Darroch Wood. Enter the wood by a stile and almost immediately turn right onto a path along the upper edge of the wood.

5 **NO162437** Meet a grassy track at the northwest corner of the wood and turn left down it. Where the track ends at a clearing continue on a path through the trees, with glimpses of Fingask Loch to the right. Beside an information board about Darroch Wood, turn right through a gate.

OPPOSITE: *Gate out of Darroch Wood (Point 6)*

6 **NO166434** Go gently downhill on a grassy track between fields towards Whitelock Farm. Walk around the right side of the farm buildings, one of which was once a mill powered by the outflow from White Loch. The track curves past an angling station on Fingask Loch then bends right at White Loch. Stay on the lane – now tarmac underfoot – to walk back to Whiteloch Avenue.

Blairgowrie Waymarked Walks are five routes around the town and are described in a leaflet. This walk joins the Bluebell Wood route, waymarked with yellow disks, at White Loch.

PERTHSHIRE
BIG TREE COUNTRY

Darroch Wood is known locally as the Bluebell Wood because these wildflowers carpet the ground. Along with smaller pink purslane, they bloom in mid to late May, creating a marvellous sight and scent. Darroch is Gaelic for oak and the wood consists largely of oak trees that have been coppiced – cut down to ground level so that several new stems grow for fuel and timber. Oakwoods provide a rich habitat for wildlife.

Muirton of Ardblair was a small weaving community and one of the last places in Scotland where strip farming took place, with each field shared among several families.

2

Comrie lies on a broad plain ringed by wooded knolls and rugged mountains. This riverside walk has stunning views of the surrounding scenery and passes ancient standing stones.

Water of Ruchill

Start	Comrie – School Road car park **NN772220**
Distance	5.6km (3.5 miles)
Grade	■ ☐ ☐ ☐ ☐
Time	1.5 to 2 hours
Terrain	Riverbank, fields and woods; earth paths and roads with pavements

Getting there: From Perth take the A85 through Crieff to Comrie. Turn right into the car park after the road bends right by the White Church.

Public transport: Bus number 15 runs roughly hourly (bi-hourly on Sundays) from Perth to Comrie and stops in the village centre near Melville Square – see (1).

The Water of Ruchill's riparian woodland and shingle banks are one of the most dynamic habitats in Perthshire. Heavy rainfall in the mountains creates sudden spates that wash away trees and sometimes flood houses. The alder trees that line the banks thrive in a damp environment and produce seed cones that float, so they readily colonise new shingle islands. Snowdrops bloom under them in February.

PERTHSHIRE
BIG TREE COUNTRY

Comrie Oakwoods SSSI can be seen to north of the village, softening the contours of Glen Lednock. They are designated a Site of Special Scientific Interest because of their rich biodiversity. In the past, the oaks were protected because of the value of their bark for tannin and wood for charcoal.

Prehistoric settlers left their mark on this area with cup-marked stones and a small 'four-poster' stone circle, and later the Romans built a fort here. Comrie is now an attractive village at the confluence of three rivers: the Earn, the Lednock and the Water of Ruchill. This walk is on flat ground around the south part of the village – known as Dalginross – and is easier than the better-known Glen Lednock Circular. It is a shortened version of the waymarked Ruchill Walk, which goes farther south around Cultybraggan, an old military training camp that has been bought by the community.

1 **NN772220** Continue along School Road from the car park and turn right by some garages along a path that leads to Melville Square in the centre of the village. Go straight across the main road, the A85, and ahead along Bridge Street. Cross Dalginross Bridge over the River Earn, with a fine view of the White Church – now a community centre – upstream. Immediately, turn right into a lane called Field of Refuge.

2 **NN773218** Go right through a gap in the fence just before a small car park (an alternative starting point). Take the earth path, which bends left into riverside woodland. After passing the confluence of the Earn and the Ruchill, the path bends left. Follow the river upstream for a mile, keeping to the path closest to the river, but diverting to the left if you come across places where it has been undercut by the river. Ignore the first sign for Cowden Road as you pass Ruchilside.

3 **NN766205** After skirting a field, turn left at the second fingerpost for Cowden Road, under a large, spreading sycamore tree. Pass a small ruin, go up a bank, and follow a path to the left along the top of the bank. At a T-junction, turn right along a drive, which soon bends left to the B827 Braco road.

4 **NN774206** Go straight across the road to a standing stone known as the Roman Stone, although the cup marks on it suggest that it was erected millennia before the Romans arrived. Follow the track ahead, enjoying wide views over fields then walking beside houses. On meeting the Cowden Road, go straight over – in the direction of Muirend – on a path between trees and a stream.

5 **NN780209** At a sign for Strowan Road, turn left over a footbridge into Poggles Wood. Follow a path through the left side of the wood to the South Crieff road, nearly opposite the end of Strowan Road. Go right a short distance to see a small stone circle on the edge of the wood, just outside the cemetery wall. Then walk back and along Strowan Road, which bends left beside the fire station taking you back to Dalginross Bridge. Retrace your steps to the start.

ABOVE: *Water of Ruchill*

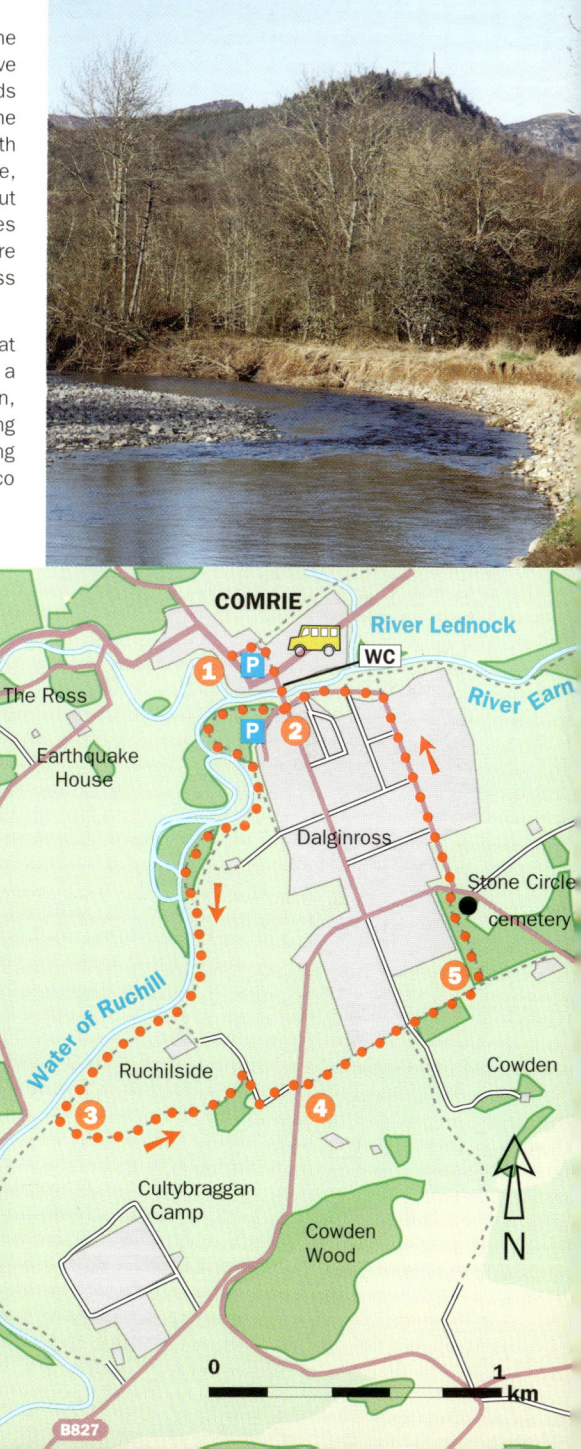

3

The historic county town of Kinross-shire lies on the edge of Scotland's largest lowland loch. Big skies and wide views enhance this easy circuit along the wildlife-rich shore.

Loch Leven and Kinross

Start	Kinross – The Pier **NO122017**
Distance	6km (3.75 miles)
Grade	■ ☐ ☐ ☐ ☐
Time	1.5 to 2 hours
Terrain	Park, woods and fields beside loch; well-surfaced paths and pavement through town.

Getting there: Follow signs for Kinross from the M90. Turn right in the centre then go third left and fork right to the pier car park.

Public transport: Many buses, from Perth and elsewhere, stop in the centre of Kinross.

Allow time to look around before beginning the walk. Historic Scotland boatmen ferry visitors from the small stone jetty at Kinross Pier to ruined Lochleven Castle on Castle Island (in summer), while Kinross Fisheries boats are kept in the little harbour. The adjacent building houses the Boathouse Bistro and the office of the Scottish Natural Heritage rangers. During the walk, please keep dogs under close control to avoid disturbing wildlife and only let them go in the water at Kirkgate Park.

1 **NO122017** Walk through the stone gateway feature marking the start of the Trail and follow the raised boardwalk through a reed bed. Cross a stream and come to the grassy expanse of Kirkgate Park, which has a large array of play equipment. Turn right along the shore, with views back to the Pier. At the end of the Park, pass the Kirkgate Watchtower and an ancient graveyard then follow its perimeter wall to a viewpoint overlooking the loch.

2 **NO128017** The view stretches over a grassy field, which is a popular roost site for geese, to Castle Island and Bishop Hill. As you continue, look out for the ornamental Fish Gate on the left, through which you can glimpse Kinross House and Gardens. Soon a wood comes between you and the loch. At a stone marker, detour a short way to the right to visit a bird hide with superb view over the loch.

3 **NO129023** Return to the main path and continue through wetlands and woods. Look out for Mary's Ponds, two shady pools with wooden viewing platforms. Beyond them the path winds through willow scrub to a stone wall. Turn left to Mary's Gate with its high pillars – like the ponds it is named after Mary Queen of Scots.

4 **NO129033** Don't go through the gate but continue past it along the edge of Kinross golf course. The path runs under a fine avenue of beech trees and curves around the north end of the fairways. At the far corner of the course, follow a path in the direction of Kinross through a gap in a wall on the right. It takes you through woodland

beside a stream to the end of a lane. Keep right on the path to continue along a woodland strip parallel to the lane.

5 **NO116033** The path joins the lane – Sunny Brae – just before a main road linking Kinross and Milnathort. Turn left along the pavement and follow the road back through Kinross, passing several hostelries and a café en route back to the Pier car park.

OPPOSITE TOP: *Loch Leven and Castle Island from the Kirkgate viewpoint (Point 2)*

OPPOSITE BOTTOM: *View through the Fish Gate to Kinross House*

Loch Leven National Nature Reserve is one of the most important sites in Britain for waterfowl and is managed by Scottish Natural Heritage. Thousands of migratory geese, ducks and swans arrive in autumn and winter to roost and feed on the reserve. The loch also attracts the largest concentration of nesting ducks in Britain, and is a haven for plants and smaller animals, such as water voles.

Loch Leven Heritage Trail was completed in 2008, giving unprecedented access to the loch shore. The full trail runs 12.5 km (8 miles) from Kinross to Vane Farm; this route leaves it at Mary's Gate. The trail's level path is well used by walkers, cyclists, people with disabilities, children and dogs. Imaginative artworks and interpretation reflect the loch's stories, from the imprisonment of Mary Queen of Scots on Castle Island to the birth of the sport of curling. For more information, please visit the website www.discoverlochleven.com.

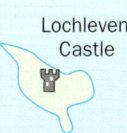

4

The Carse of Gowrie coastal plain is home to many historic orchards. This walk from Errol village crosses pancake-flat farmland to one at Port Allen on the edge of the Tay reed beds.

Errol and Port Allen

Start	Errol – Mercat Cross, High Street **NO250227**
Distance	8km (5 miles); shorter walk 5.6km (3.5 miles)
Grade	■ ☐ ☐ ☐ ☐
Time	2.5 hours (shorter walk 1.5 hours)
Terrain	Fields and woods fringing the Tay reed beds; surfaced tracks and earth paths

Getting there: Follow signs for Errol from the A90 Perth to Dundee dual carriageway

Public transport: Bus numbers 16 and 54 between Perth and Dundee stop at Errol Cross, providing a roughly hourly service.

Errol lies between the Sidlaw Hills and the Firth of Tay, at the heart of the rich farmland of the Carse of Gowrie. A deep channel, the Pow of Errol, drains the fields between village and sea. This circuit runs beside the Pow and through woods fringing the Tay reed beds to Port Allen, where the burn meets the estuary. For a shorter walk, head straight to Tay Lodge and omit the eastern section.

Carse of Gowrie Historic Orchards date back 800 years and were established by medieval abbeys that owned farms in the area. Bloody Ploughman, Lass o' Gowrie and Tower of Glamis are among the many heritage varieties of apples first grown here. Port Allen is one of the largest surviving orchards. It still has approximately 80 veteran trees, including apples, pears and plums, which produce good quality fruit.

The Carse of Gowrie Group is working with other partners to promote and restore the historic orchards, which have suffered a century of neglect. The Group is also developing path networks around the communities of the Carse and the Sidlaws – the range of hills to the north. See www.cogg.org.uk for other routes.

1 **NO250227** From the unicorn-topped Mercat Cross, walk down Gas Brae, to the left of the Old Smiddy pub. At the edge of the houses, keep straight ahead past a barrier and down a narrow lane. Young apple trees have been planted on the banks. The lane slopes downhill, then flattens out on the flood plain of the Tay. Immediately after going over a bridge with low parapets, you come to a crossroads of well-surfaced tracks.

2 **NO256224** *For the shorter version of the walk, go straight ahead to Tay Lodge (4).* For the full route, turn left to walk beside the Pow of Errol. Ahead is a line of poplars with Dundee off to their right. Pass a pumping station and continue to a junction level with the poplars where you keep straight ahead. Farther on, the track curves right towards the tree-lined estuary.

3 **NO269229** Where the main track bends left towards a sewage works, turn right on a newly surfaced path. It soon enters a linear wood of oak, beech, sycamore, birch, cherry, aspen and other broadleaved trees. Follow the beaten earth path along the top of a bank that drops down to the Tay reed beds on the left. For 1.4km (nearly 1 mile), you walk through a tunnel of trees then the path bends right to the outer edge of the trees and runs to a junction at Tay Lodge.

4 **NO259222** Walk around a barrier then go right on a path that continues through the trees bordering the estuary. Pass Daleally Farm, just visible through a hedge, and later enjoy an open view over the Tay.

Shortly before Port Allen, a lagoon on the left provides a haven for ducks, coots, herons and gulls. Now there is a drop off on both sides of the path, with the Pow on the right and the lagoon on the left. A good view over the water to Newburgh in Fife appears as you leave the trees then the path bends right across a bridge over the Pow.

5 **NO250212** Follow the path up a grassy rise and straight on between Port Allen Cottage and the adjacent farm steading. Port Allen orchard is over to your left. Follow a tarmac lane away from the Tay and turn right at the first track (opposite a cottage). Keep on to a T-junction and turn right towards Daleally Farm. Before the buildings, fork left to skirt the farm then go left again to walk beside the Pow of Errol once more. Continue to the crossroads of tracks and turn left to return into Errol village.

OPPOSITE: *The Mercat Cross in Errol (Point 1)*

5

Waterfalls, woodland and wide views to the mountains make this one of the finest walks in Highland Perthshire.

Birks of Aberfeldy and Dunskaig

Start	Aberfeldy – the Square **NN856490**
Distance	6.4km (4 miles)
Grade	■ ■ ☐ ☐ ☐
Time	2 to 2.5 hours
Terrain	Wooded gorge where path with many steps runs beside fenced steep drops; then good tracks through pasture

Getting there: Leave the A9 at Ballinluig and follow the A827 to the centre of Aberfeldy

Public transport: Regular buses from Perth and elsewhere stop at Chapel Street by the Square

The Moness Burn runs through Aberfeldy, where it used to power the Watermill, which is now a bookshop, café and gallery. This walk runs through the Lower Birks to the Upper Birks where paths circuit a gorge. After climbing up the side of the ravine with the best views, this walk returns more gently downhill through birchwood and pastures overlooking Aberfeldy.

The **Birks of Aberfeldy** is a spectacular gorge named after a song by Robert Burns, Scotland's national poet. He visited in 1787 and was inspired by the towering rock walls of the Moness Burn and its high, foaming waterfall. 'Birks' is Scots for birch trees, and delightful birch woodland still grows around the upper part of the gorge. A wide range of exotic specimen trees grows in a **Tree Collection** beside the Upper Birks car park.

BIG TREE COUNTRY

Weem Wood can be seen across the valley on the second half of the walk. This ancient woodland covers a craggy hillside on the opposite side of Strath Tay, beyond the historic Wade Bridge. It has a picnic site and a 1 mile waymarked walk.

1 **NN856490** Walk from the Square along Bridge End, in the direction of Kenmore, and turn left before the bridge over Moness Burn to go under a war memorial arch. Walk through the Lower Birks and fork right over a footbridge. After going up steps and over a mill lade, keep left to cross the A826 by traffic lights at the road bridge. Walk ahead through the Upper Birks car park, or though the Tree Collection on the right.

2 **NN855484** Take the path ahead at the top of the car park, walking under mature beech trees. Soon turn left over a footbridge to follow the east path all the way to the top. After passing a seated statue of Robert Burns, enter the gorge and go left up steps to cross a bridge over a waterfall. Burn's Seat is on the left before the path zigzags up to a higher level. Come to a viewpoint looking across to the high Falls of Moness.

3 **NN852472** The path soon bends right to cross a footbridge over the top of the falls, where the water cascades into thin air. Turn left for Urlar on the far side along a path

that continues up the gorge before bending right through birch woodland. Come to the Urlar Road and turn right downhill then go left in 70m (75 yards) through a multi-user gate on to a track.

4 **NN850474** The track runs diagonally downhill through a mix of pasture and open birch woodland. Farragon Hill and Meall Tairneachan are the two summits across the strath. After going through a gate halfway down there is a fine view of conical Schiehallion ahead. Beyond a gate in a stone wall, join another track and head more steeply downhill. Above Dunskaig – a farm steading converted into houses – turn right.

5 **NN839481** The track runs on a level back towards Aberfeldy, soon passing through the stone wall again. It becomes tarmac after crossing a burn by the Heart of Scotland wood and eventually meets the Urlar Road at a T-junction. Turn left downhill and at the junction with the A826 go straight over and down steps. Retrace your route through the Lower Birks back to the Square.

OPPOSITE TOP: *The Square, Aberfeldy (Point 1)*

OPPOSITE BOTTOM: *The Falls of Moness from the viewpoint (Point 3)*

BELOW: *Robert Burns statue*

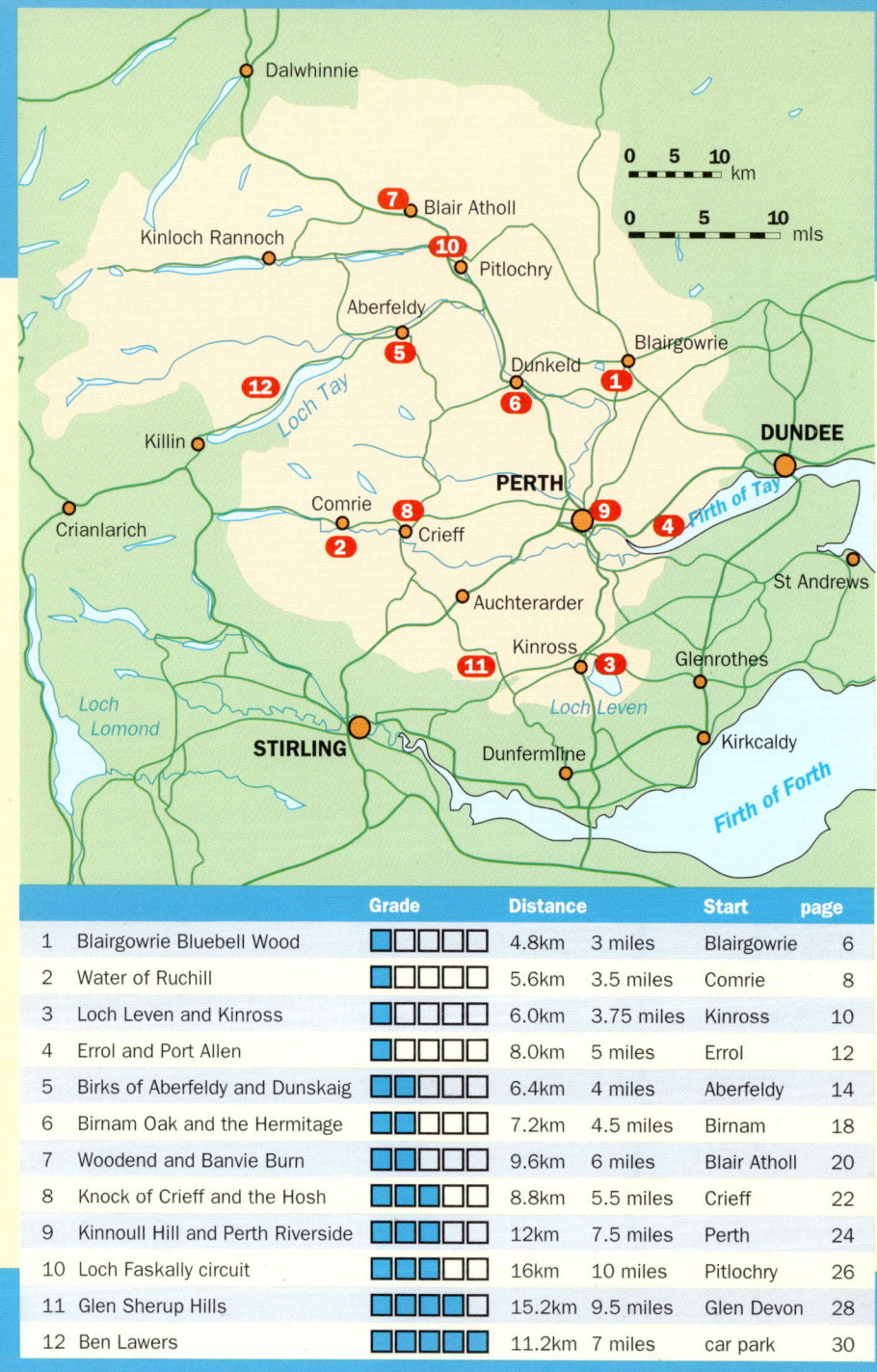

		Grade	Distance		Start	page
1	Blairgowrie Bluebell Wood	■□□□□	4.8km	3 miles	Blairgowrie	6
2	Water of Ruchill	■□□□□	5.6km	3.5 miles	Comrie	8
3	Loch Leven and Kinross	■□□□□	6.0km	3.75 miles	Kinross	10
4	Errol and Port Allen	■□□□□	8.0km	5 miles	Errol	12
5	Birks of Aberfeldy and Dunskaig	■■□□□	6.4km	4 miles	Aberfeldy	14
6	Birnam Oak and the Hermitage	■■□□□	7.2km	4.5 miles	Birnam	18
7	Woodend and Banvie Burn	■■■□□	9.6km	6 miles	Blair Atholl	20
8	Knock of Crieff and the Hosh	■■■□□	8.8km	5.5 miles	Crieff	22
9	Kinnoull Hill and Perth Riverside	■■■□□	12km	7.5 miles	Perth	24
10	Loch Faskally circuit	■■■□□	16km	10 miles	Pitlochry	26
11	Glen Sherup Hills	■■■■□	15.2km	9.5 miles	Glen Devon	28
12	Ben Lawers	■■■■■	11.2km	7 miles	car park	30

Walk information

The walk grade reflects the amount of climbing involved, the quality of the paths and the nature of the terrain.

■☐☐☐☐ gentle
■■■■■ strenuous

For each walk description, grid references are given (in grey) for the start point and for each numbered route point, as shown on the adjacent map. These can be used is conjunction with an Ordnance Survey map if you wish, or as GPS waypoints. The time given is an approximate indication of how long it will take, allowing for some brief stops – you may go faster or slower.

Safety in the hills

This guide includes a map of every route, but for walks in the higher hills and mountains graded as ■■■■☐ or as ■■■■■, you are strongly advised to carry a compass and full-sized map, which will show you more of the surrounding area and help with navigation if you stray from the route.

For the more demanding routes, you should carry adequate equipment for your comfort and safety: a full set of waterproofs, spare warm clothing, food and drink, torch and a whistle. Weather can change very rapidly in the hills and the summits are usually colder and windier than the start point. It is also sensible to let someone know when and where you are going, and your expected return time.

Key to walk maps 1 – 12

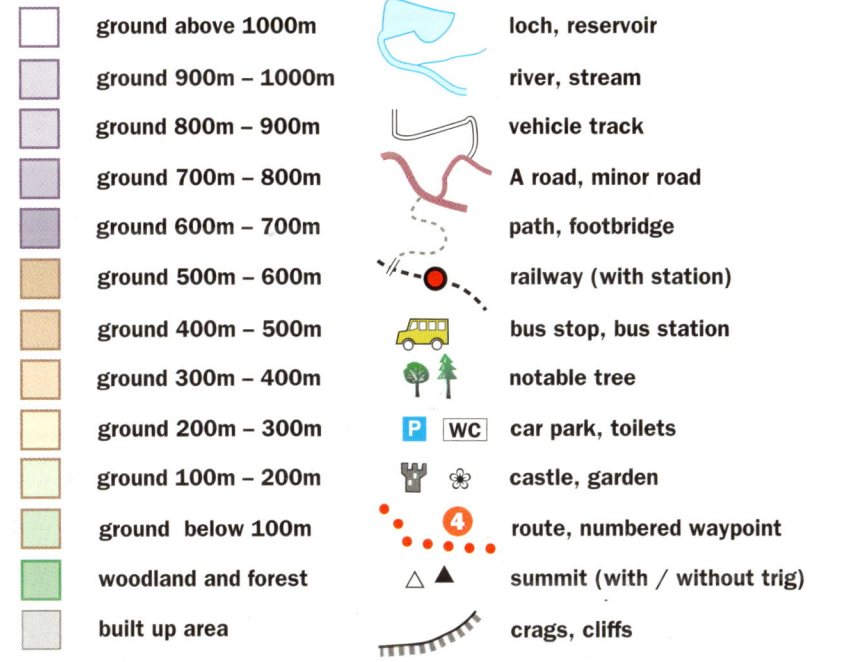

ground above 1000m	loch, reservoir
ground 900m – 1000m	river, stream
ground 800m – 900m	vehicle track
ground 700m – 800m	A road, minor road
ground 600m – 700m	path, footbridge
ground 500m – 600m	railway (with station)
ground 400m – 500m	bus stop, bus station
ground 300m – 400m	notable tree
ground 200m – 300m	car park, toilets
ground 100m – 200m	castle, garden
ground below 100m	route, numbered waypoint
woodland and forest	summit (with / without trig)
built up area	crags, cliffs

6

Dunkeld and Birnam lie amid wooded hills at the heart of Big Tree Country. This landscape is the legacy of the Dukes of Atholl, who planted millions of trees for pleasure and profit.

Birnam Oak and the Hermitage

Start	Birnam – Beatrix Potter Garden **NO031418**
Distance	7.2km (4.5 miles)
Grade	☐☐☐☐☐
Time	2.5 hours
Terrain	Wooded riverbanks and conifer forest; good tracks and paths

Getting there: The Beatrix Potter Garden is opposite the Birnam Hotel in the centre of Birnam; turn off the A9 at signs for Birnam and Dunkeld.

Public transport: Buses from Perth and elsewhere stop at the start, which is a short walk from Birnam railway station.

The **Birnam Oak** is an ancient tree, whose limbs are supported by crutches. Legend is that it is a remnant of Birnam Wood, which Shakespeare immortalised in his play Macbeth. The adjacent **Birnam Sycamore,** a faster-growing species, is a similar size, but only about 300 years old.

PERTHSHIRE

BIG TREE COUNTRY

The Hermitage is a woodland garden first laid out 250 years ago when the Dukes of Atholl had a big house at Dunkeld. It contains a stone summerhouse with a balcony overlooking the Black Linn waterfall. Called Ossian's Hall, it was built in 1758 as a memorial to Ossian, a 3rd century blind bard. Red squirrels are frequently seen around the Hermitage.

The **Hermitage Douglas** fir, despite being relatively young, is one of the tallest trees in Britain.

The **Beatrix Potter Garden** has bronze statues of the author's characters. The area's natural history fascinated her during childhood holidays spent here, and inspired her stories and illustrations. The adjacent Birnam Institute, a community arts and conference centre, houses the Beatrix Potter exhibition and a café.

Birnam and Dunkeld have a well-established path network with walks waymarked by coloured posts. This route follows parts of four of those walks on a loop that links the area's two most famous trees.

1 NO031418 Walk to the right of the Birnam Hotel down Oak Road, which bends right into a play park. Keep left down steps to the riverside path and turn left – upstream – through the woodland beside the Tay.

2 NO033420 Soon come to an information board about 'a living legend', the Birnam Oak. The next tree beside the path is 'the young pretender', the Birnam Sycamore. Beyond a footbridge, the path runs closer to the river with views across the water to Dunkeld. Go under the Telford Bridge and some fine tall trees – a taste of what's to come at the Hermitage. The path bends left by the confluence of the Tay and Braan. At a T-junction, go right under the A9 road bridge then across a wooden footbridge over the Braan.

3 NO022421 Follow the track ahead, pass Forestry Commission Tay Forest District offices and turn right through Inver. When the road ends, continue beside the A9 then turn left into the Hermitage. Walk through the lower car park and go under a railway arch by the river. Keep on the path beside the Braan to a grove of tall Douglas fir and a viewpoint by the Black Linn pool looking across to the Hermitage Douglas. Go up steps to the Hermitage Bridge, but before crossing visit Ossian's Hall on the right for a view of the Black Linn waterfall from the balcony.

4 NO008417 Beyond the bridge, pass the Hermitage Douglas to another viewpoint looking back towards it. The path contours above the Braan, which drops away in a series of rapids, then curves up to the Inver car park. Go up steps and walk right for a short distance then turn left at black and yellow posts onto a rough track. Head uphill to a road with faster traffic, the A822, and go straight across it and into Ladywell Forest.

5 NO016417 Walk uphill on the broad forest road, going round a sharp left bend before a wide junction of tracks. Stay on the middle track, which curves right uphill through the forest. At another large junction, turn left, now more on the level. Turn left again at the next junction then immediately go right on to a small path leading down to a burn.

6 NO020410 Cross the Inchewan Burn by a footbridge and turn left down the track beyond. Walk downhill through the deciduous woodland, with Birnam Hill rising steeply above on your right. When the track forks lower down, go right, briefly uphill. Keep straight ahead and go across a minor road to houses, continuing down the path beyond. Walk under the railway line (steps to the right lead to the station) and under the A9 road bridge, immediately turning right between road and houses. Then turn left, past the Birnam Institute, back to the start point.

OPPOSITE: *The Black Linn waterfall from the balcony of Ossian's Hall (Point 4)*

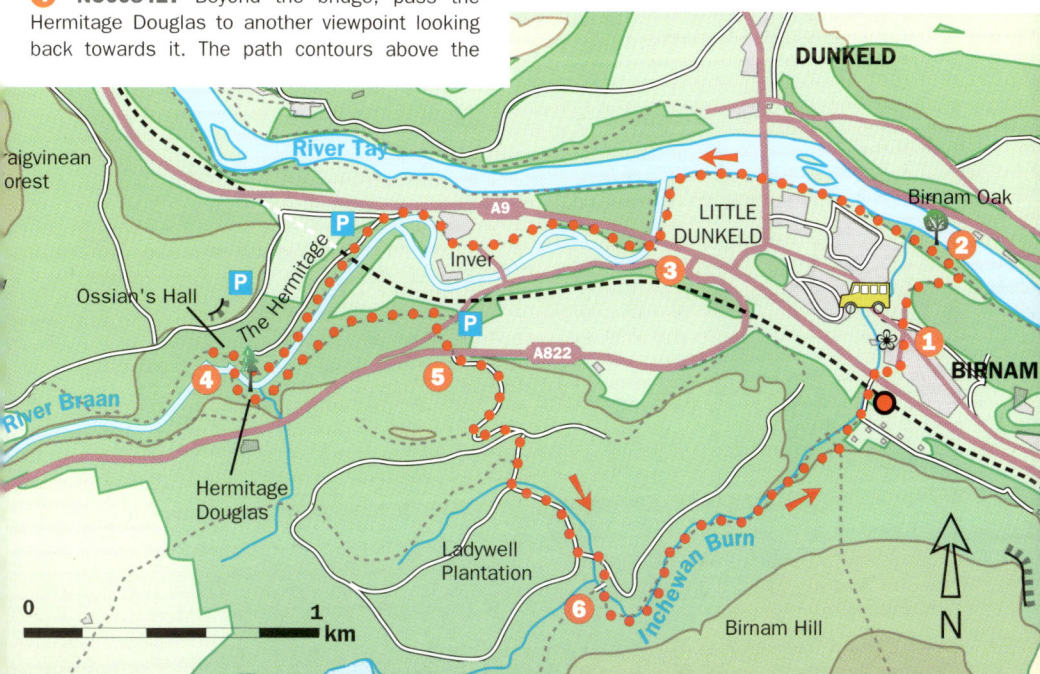

7

Delightfully landscaped parkland and woodland surround Blair Castle, the focal point of the village of Blair Atholl. The views are enchanting and the woods abound with red squirrels.

Woodend and Banvie Burn

Start	Blair Atholl – Glen Tilt car park **NN874662**
Distance	9.6km (6 miles)
Grade	■ ■ □ □ □
Time	3 hours
Terrain	Fields and woods; good tracks and a short section of tarmac

Getting there: From Perth take the A9 north, turn off into Blair Atholl and go right following signs to the Glen Tilt car park.

Public transport: If coming to Blair Atholl by train or bus, head for the grand gates leading to Blair Castle, take the path on their right, walk up the avenue and turn first right to Glen Tilt car park.

Blair Atholl is the southern gateway to the Cairngorms. The village is the hub of Atholl Estates, which encompass 145,000 acres of Highland Perthshire. The Atholl Estates Ranger Service has waymarked several trails around the area. This route largely follows the Woodend Walk, but goes farther up the wooded glen of Banvie Burn.

1 NN874662 Turn left out of the car park entrance and walk gently uphill on a lane between fields. Go left at a crossroads and walk through Old Blair. The road bends right past Diana's Grove, which is enclosed by a wall with a small gate halfway along it (opposite the start of a track).

2 NN865665 Keep straight on to a T-junction by the pony trekking centre and turn right up a splendid avenue of redwoods. You can see the Whim folly directly ahead between the trees; it was built to be an eye-catching feature from Blair Castle. At the top of the avenue, the track bends left and runs through lovely parkland with views down to the castle. Follow it for 2km (1.25 miles), passing a horseshoe-shaped pond and some ancient oak trees.

3 NN843660 At a junction of tracks, turn sharp right, signed for Bruar Falls. Keep right at the next junction (away from Bruar Falls), following blue waymarks. The track rises gently uphill through mainly larch woodland, which looks glorious in autumn, when the needles of this deciduous conifer turn golden before dropping for the winter. Watch out also for some Scots pine with remarkably tall, straight trunks.

Diana's Grove is an arboretum of giant conifers in the grounds of Blair Castle, the ancestral home of the Dukes of Atholl. Named after the Roman goddess of hunting, it contains many trees more than 150ft (45.7m) high, including a Grand fir that is the second tallest tree in Britain. If you wish to visit Diana's Grove, you can start the walk from the castle car park (when the castle is open) and go through the gate at the top of Diana's Grove to join the walk at (2). Blair Castle is open daily in summer, and on Tuesdays and Saturdays in winter. Tickets can be bought for the grounds only, and access to them is free in winter.

The **Atholl Glens** extend north from Blair Atholl into the Cairngorms and offer longer, wilder walks. Old rights of way up Glen Tilt and Glen Bruar run through to Braemar and Kingussie respectively.

4 NN855674 Higher up, the track bends left to a T-junction above Banvie Burn. Turn left along a fairly level track, following the burn upstream. Soon fork right then cross Banvie Burn by an old stone bridge, where there is a view upstream across open moorland.

5 NN853677 Follow the track, which angles uphill to the right, and keep right on joining a track above. At a fork go right again to continue downhill closer to the burn. The track runs past some impressively tall conifers – Sitka and Norway spruce, Grand and Douglas fir – to the lower bridge. Turn right over the bridge then left down the glen, high above the burn.

6 NN861671 Look out for a right turn and divert along it 250m (275yds) to the Whim, which has a panoramic view over Blair Castle to Ben Vrackie beyond. Return to the junction and continue downhill on the track. It steepens after bending right by a house and runs beside mature beech trees to the T-junction at **2**. Turn left and return along the road to the car park.

OPPOSITE: *The Whim (near Point 6)*

OPPOSITE BOTTOM: *Tall Scots pine and larch woodland (after Point 3)*

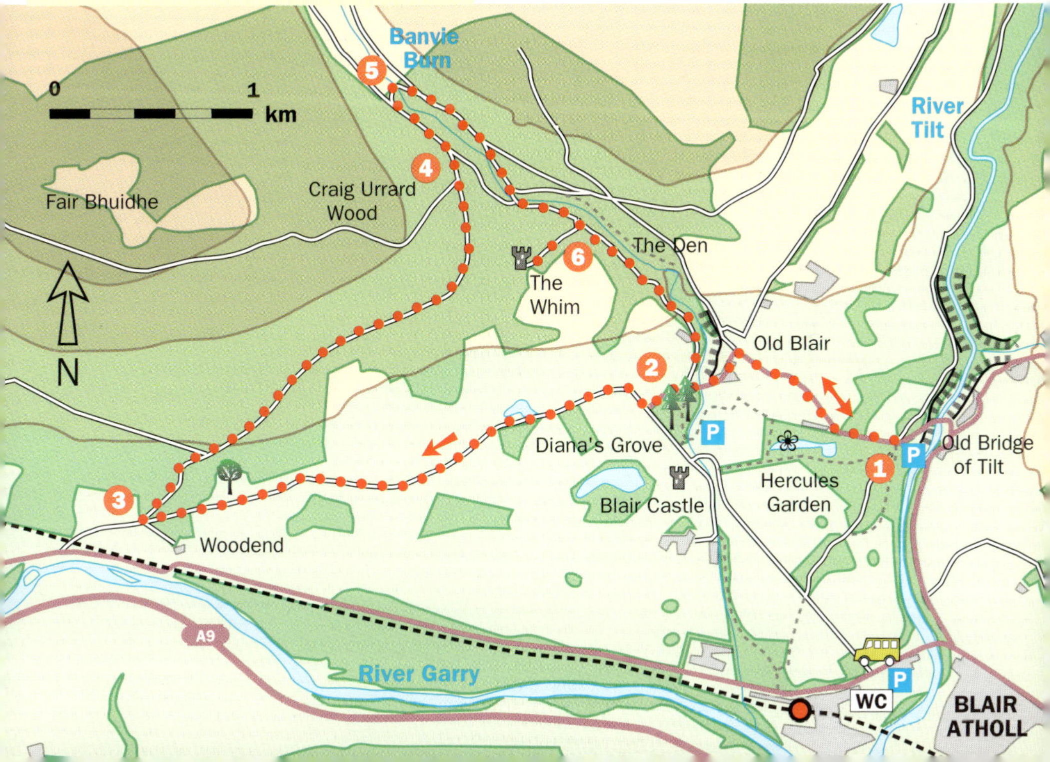

8

This walk links Crieff Hydro Hotel and the Famous Grouse Experience, Crieff's two best known institutions. The contrasting views in different directions are some of the most striking in Perthshire.

Knock of Crieff and the Hosh

Start	Crieff – Lower Knock parking area **NN864225**
Distance	8.8km (5.5 miles)
Grade	☑ ☑ ☑ ☐ ☐
Time	3 hours
Terrain	Woods, fields and open hilltop; paths and tracks with wide views

Getting there: Crieff is on the A85 from Perth. Opposite James Square, go up Hill Street, ahead along Ferntower Road then left at the top past Crieff Hydro Stables.

Public transport: Bus stop in James Square.

BELOW: *Summit of the Knock*

The Knock rises to 278m (911ft) above Crieff, a resort town on the boundary between the Highlands and Lowlands. The wooded hill offers dramatic views northwards up Glen Turret to Ben Chonzie and a gentler panorama southwards over flatter, more fertile Strathearn.

BIG TREE COUNTRY

Crieff Waymarked Walks provide a network of paths through the countryside around the town. This route begins along part of the blue-marked Knock Walk then follows the red-marked Hosh circuit through the outlying hamlet of that name.

Refreshments are available at two places on this walk. The Crieff Hydro Hotel, a popular destination for family holidays, has an idyllic setting on the slopes of the Knock. Glen Turret at the Hosh is Scotland's oldest distillery and the home of the Famous Grouse Experience.

1 **NN864225** From the Lower Knock parking bays take the path beside the walks information board. Walk uphill through broadleaved woodland to the open summit of the Knock, where there is a viewpoint indicator on a plinth. Go straight over the summit, down across a heathery dip, and up to a deer fence.

2 **NN869232** Cross a stile and go through a recently felled area to another stile on the far side – or if a diversion is in place, follow it left around the outer edge of the fence. Continue ahead up a steep, stony path into dense conifers. The gradient soon eases and the path runs through dense spruce forest past a small cairn, marking the Upper Knock summit. It continues downhill and bends left to join a forest track. Go right along

it then turn left at a bend, onto a path between two deer fences.

3 **NN877238** Where the path bends left, go through a gate onto a knoll for a birds-eye view over Monzie Castle and parkland. Return to the path and continue over a rise, soon returning to the forest track. Turn right and walk gently downhill for 1.3km (0.8 miles) past the Upper Knock car park to a junction.

4 **NN863227** Turn sharp right in the Hosh direction on a tarmac lane past various Crieff Hydro activities, including a high ropes adventure course. Beyond Culcrieff Golf Centre, walk through the Activity Centre car park and keep ahead down a stony track with open views. After passing large beech trees, the track winds downhill to a ford and footbridge across the Shaggie Burn. Continue to a minor road and turn left across a bridge. Soon turn left into Glenturret Distillery, home of the Famous Grouse Experience.

5 **NN856234** Walk through the car park and follow signs for Woodland Walks across a footbridge over the Turret Burn. Rise uphill on a woodland path then turn right to walk downstream. Leave this path, known locally as Lovers' Walk, by going left at a footpath sign for Culcrieff. Zigzag uphill to a tarmac lane. Turn left towards the Crieff Hydro self-catering lodges at Culcrieff, the site of an old estate farm.

6 **NN860231** Go right onto a marked path just before the lodges and, above them, keep straight ahead on a track through trees. Turn right at a T-junction and after leaving the wood pass the Jesus Well, dated 1874. Superb views stretch westwards up Strathearn towards Comrie and Ben Vorlich, and later southwards over Crieff. Come to a tarmac lane and keep straight ahead along it.

7 **NN864223** Just before the lane runs through a high wall to the Crieff Hydro Hotel, turn left through a kissing gate and walk up the side of a pony field. Beyond another gate, keep ahead on a tarmac drive past more lodges to return to the Lower Knock parking area.

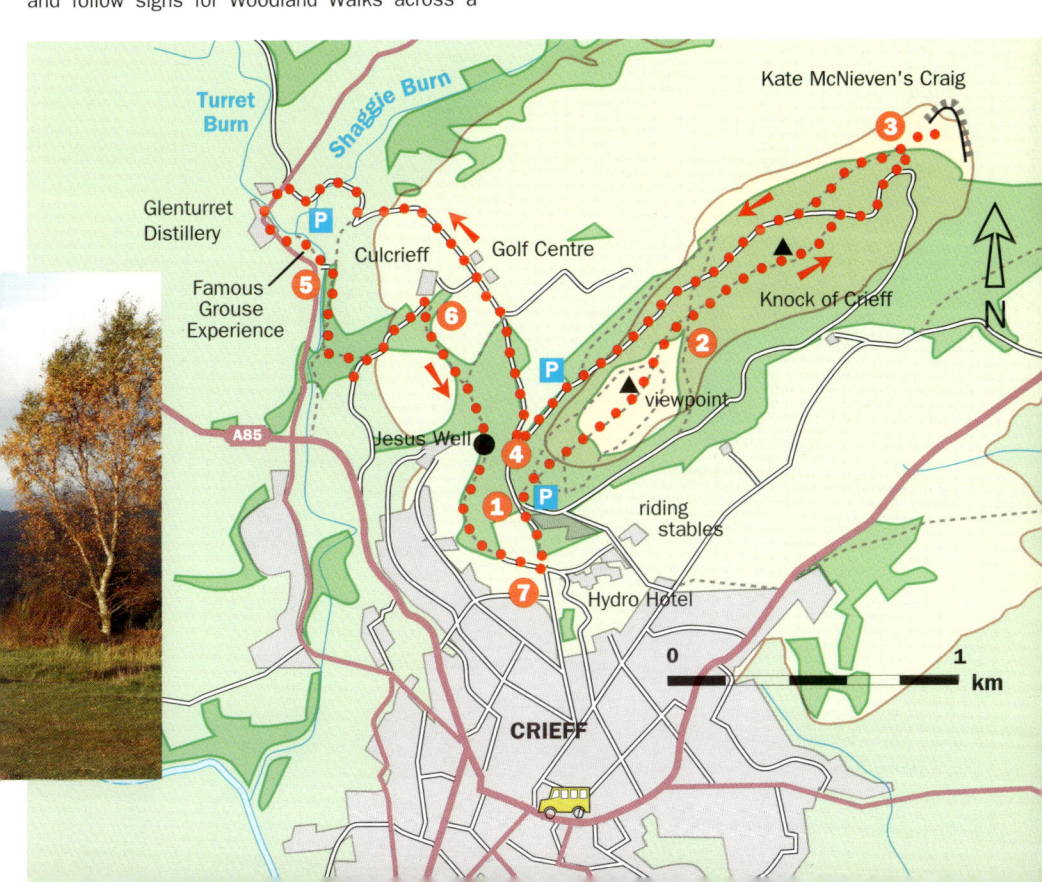

9

Perth has an idyllic setting on the mighty River Tay, Britain's largest river. This circuit follows paths up the wooded hill on its outskirts and back through delightful riverside gardens.

Kinnoull Hill and Perth Riverside

Start	Perth – South Inch **NO120230**
Distance	12km (7.5 miles)
Grade	☐☐☐☐☐
Time	3.5 to 4 hours
Terrain	Parks and wooded hills with cliffs; good paths and tarmac pavements

Getting there: The South Inch car park (pay and display) is on the A912, Edinburgh Road, on the south edge of the city centre

Public transport: Perth bus and rail stations are on Leonard Street; walk along the edge of the South Inch to the start.

This walk starting from the centre of Perth offers great views. It is suitable for any season, but care should be taken near the cliffs – especially in winter when paths may be slippery.

1 **NO120230** From the South Inch car park entrance, cross the road and turn left. Walk under a railway bridge and immediately go up steps onto a gangway on the railway viaduct over the River Tay. Pass above Moncreiffe Island and, on the far side, follow the path enclosed by a high wall up to the Dundee Road. Cross the busy road and go up the lane on the right. Bend left at the entrance to Branklyn Garden then at a crossroads turn right along Fairmount Terrace.

2 **NO125224** Fork left up a track then continue on a path going uphill beside a hedge. Keep ahead past a sign for Kinnoull Hill Woodland Park. The path climbs above the rising cliffs of Kinnoull Hill, with a sheer drop on the right. It levels off by a bench overlooking Friarton Bridge then bends left

and crosses a grassy area to another bench. Go right uphill to a T-junction and turn right along a wider path. Crest a rise and continue downhill into a small valley then up steps to a junction.

3 **NO133226** Bear right on a path that soon bends left and climbs to a junction beside a picnic table. Turn right towards the summit, going right again at a crossroads. Reach a stone table in a grassy area at the top. The route continues ahead, but first enjoy the panorama over the cliffs on the right and walk left to the trig point and a viewpoint indicator that identifies many mountains to the north.

4 **NO139227** Keep on above the cliffs to Kinnoull Tower, then continue on the clifftop path to a T-junction. Turn right and follow a track downhill then around a field, ignoring all left turns. Cross a minor road to the Jubilee car park and the Jim Aitken Arboretum. Walk through the car park and go right uphill on a stony track.

5 NO148237 Beyond a gate turn left onto a path around a forested hill. At a marker post turn left downhill through tall Scots pines. Go through a metal gate and turn left down Coronation Road, following it all the way to a road at the bottom.

6 NO138251 Turn left at the road on to the Milkboys Path, following it across fields back to Perth. Join Gannochy Road and continue ahead along it for 1km (0.8 miles), passing the Murray Royal Hospital. At a T-junction, turn right down Lochie Brae.

7 NO122239 At trafic lights, go diagonally over the crossroads and walk to the left along the pavement. Beyond flats, go down steps into the riverside park. Pass through a gap in a wall and follow the path closest to the river. Walk under Queen's Bridge and continue beside the river to the railway viaduct. Turn sharp right to cross it and return to the start.

OPPOSITE: *Kinnoull Tower (Point 4) stands above the River Tay*

Kinnoull Hill Woodland Park covers the hills that rise above Perth to dramatic cliffs overlooking the River Tay. Walk through natural deciduous woodland on Kinnoull Hill and mature Scots pine plantation in Deuchny Wood. Pass Kinnoull Tower, a romantic folly perched on the cliff edge, and the Jim Aitken Arboretum, created with a bequest from this well-known local landscape gardener. The route returns down the Coronation Road, so named because Scottish monarchs trod it on their way to Scone, the traditional place of enthronement.

Perth Riverside is a green corridor that you follow through the city. A Sculpture Trail runs through the gardens lining the east bank of the River Tay: Bellwood Park, Rodney Gardens and Norrie Miller Walk. Nearby is Branklyn Garden, a plant enthusiast's paradise.

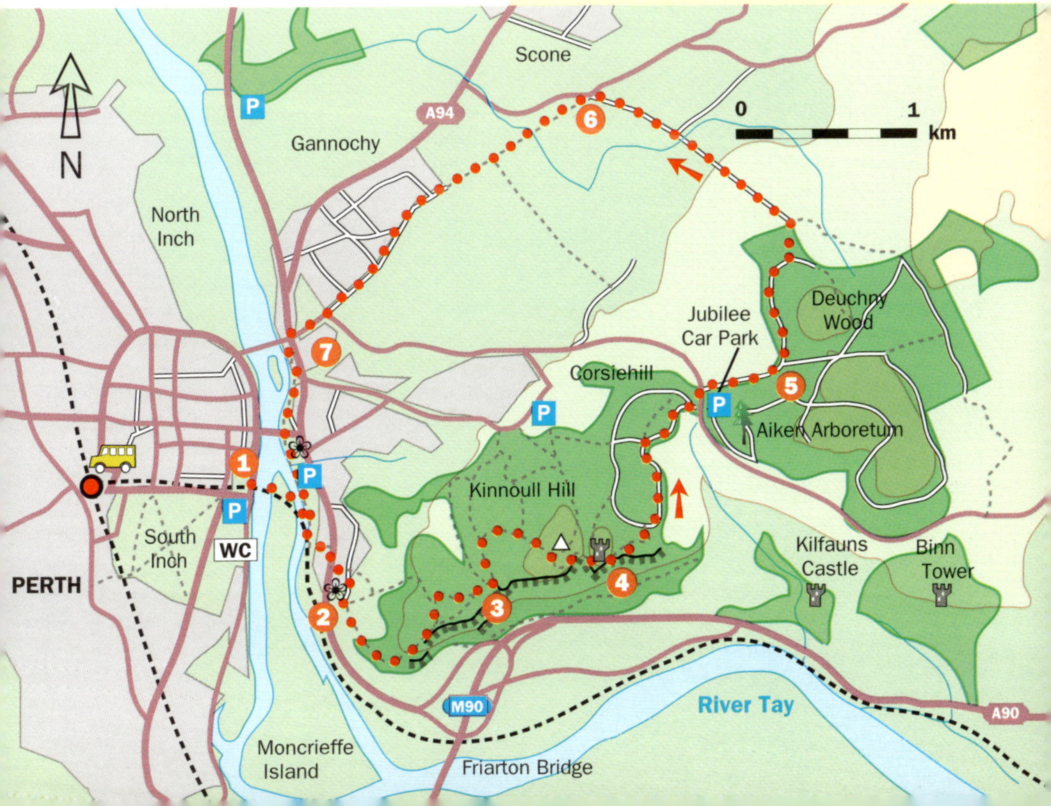

PERTHSHIRE
BIG
TREE
COUNTRY

10

Loch Faskally sets off the surrounding woods and mountains beautifully. It looks natural, but was created in 1950 when Pitlochry Dam was built as part of a vast hydroelectric scheme.

Loch Faskally circuit

Start	Pitlochry – Atholl Road car park **NN941580**
Distance	16km (10 miles); shorter walk 5.6km (3.5 miles)
Grade	■ ■ ■ ☐ ☐
Time	5 hours
Terrain	Woods and meadows around the loch; paths and roads

Getting there: Turn off the A9 into Pitlochry; the car park is beside the visitor information centre.

Public transport: Regular train and bus services to Pitlochry.

The **Explorers Garden,** above Pitlochry Festival Theatre, pays tribute to Scottish plant collectors, including those who introduced many of our forest trees from North America.

PERTHSHIRE
BIG TREE COUNTRY

Pitlochry Salmon Ladder enables fish to bypass Pitlochry Dam and Power Station to reach Loch Faskally and the rivers Tummel and Garry.

The **Linn of Tummel** is an impressive fall, although it was much higher before Loch Faskally raised the water level downstream. The **Pass of Killiecrankie,** a spectacular wooded gorge, was the site of the 1689 battle where the Jacobite leader 'Bonnie Dundee' was mortally wounded.

Faskally Wood has been carefully managed to create a beautiful landscape of mixed woodland with trees up to 200 years old. It is part of Tay Forest Park and the venue of the annual Enchanted Forest event.

A network of Pitlochry Waymarked Walks radiates out from the town. This route follows the blue-marked Killiecrankie route beside the loch to (4) and returns down the other side along parts of the green-marked Bealach route.

1 **NN941580** Turn right along the High Street then go second left, by a metal fingerpost, down Burnside Road and through an arch under the railway (where a ramp leads down from the station). Keep ahead, cross a road and go up a track into Bobbin Mill Wood. Fork right at the top of a rise onto a path down to a road. Go straight over, down to and across the Port na Craig suspension bridge.

2 **NN940576** Turn right past Pitlochry Festival Theatre and up a path on the left side of the salmon ladder to the top of Pitlochry Dam. Follow the shore path beside Loch Faskally with views to Ben Vrackie. Beyond steps, continue on a higher tarmac path and go through a gate. Turn right down the Clunie Road, go under the A9 flyover and pass the Clunie Footbridge. For the shorter walk go across it and continue from (7).

3 **NN927585** Follow the quiet road high above Loch Faskally with views to Faskally Wood. Come to fields and walk past the Priest's Stone, a standing stone carved with a cross. Beyond, the road bends left past the Clunie Arch and Power Station and you can see up the Pass of Killiecrankie to the mountain Carn Liath. Continue for 1km (0.8 miles) above the River Tummel then turn right for Killiecrankie, going down across the Coronation footbridge.

4 NN903601 Turn right, downstream, and keep ahead until the path bends left where the Tummel meets Loch Faskally. Here, you can divert right down steps to an obelisk commemorating Queen Victoria's visit in 1844 then scramble upstream to a Linn of Tummel falls viewpoint. Return to the path and continue up the River Garry arm of the loch, going down steps to a beach

OPPOSITE: *View across Loch Faskally to Faskally Wood*

under tall trees. After going under the high Garry Bridge, keep ahead to a footbridge across the Pass of Killiecrankie.

5 NN914612 Turn right on the far side of the river and walk under Garry Bridge again. The path bends left up a little valley to a junction where you turn right to continue around fields, By buildings, join a lane and go right along it. Walk around a bay into Faskally Wood and turn second right to Loch Dunmore.

6 NN919592 Walk along the left shore of the pretty little loch then cross the wooden Chinese Bridge and turn left down the far side. Go around the foot of the loch then turn sharp right on an uphill path. Turn left at a path junction and keep right at the next. The path zigzags down steps to run along the shore of Loch Faskally past a stone viewpoint to the Clunie Footbridge.

7 NN927586 Continue under the A9 flyover to the Boathouse and go right up a road. Beyond the Green Hotel, turn right back to the loch. Follow the shore path through oakwood and past a beach to Pitlochry Dam. Turn left up a lane, past the rail station and under the railway line to Rieachan car park. Turn left, then right to return down the High Street to the start.

11

Two long ridges around Glen Sherup give grassy, high-level walking. The views are among the best in the Ochils, ranging from Highland Munros to the Pentland Hills beyond the Forth.

Glen Sherup hills

Start	Glen Devon – Glensherup Forest car park **NN972051**
Distance	15.2km (9.5 miles)
Grade	☐☐☐☐☐
Time	5 hours
Terrain	Forest; open hills with young trees on their slopes; tracks and paths
Ascent	500m (1640ft)

Getting there: Take the A823 through Glen Devon and turn into the car park 2km (1.5 miles) northwest of Glendevon village.

Public transport: Bus no. 606 runs through the glen from Auchterarder morning and afternoon on school days.

Glen Devon bisects the long range of rounded Ochil Hills. Dams across the River Devon and its tributaries have created several reservoirs that supply water to central Scotland. The Woodland Trust has planted new native woodland on the south side of the glen, around Glen Sherup and Glen Quey, to link with Forestry Commission's existing Glensherup Forest. The recently erected Green Knowes wind turbines are on the hills to the north.

PERTHSHIRE **BIG TREE** COUNTRY

The waymarked **Reservoirs Trail** is a linear route linking four reservoirs.

ABOVE: *North ridge of Innerdownie*
OPPOSITE: *Tarmangie Hill*

This route follows part of the Reservoirs Trail, but climbs above it onto Innerdownie for a circuit of Glen Sherup via Tarmangie Hill and Ben Shee. Make sure you are adequately equipped for this long walk over open, exposed hilltops.

1 **NN972051** Start along the path beside Glensherup Burn and join the track leading into the forest. A gap in the Sitka spruce allows a view across to Ben Shee and Glensherup Dam, which are on the return route. Keep left at a wide junction and walk uphill through trees to the head of a burn valley where there is a large felled area above the track. Shortly after re-entering trees, turn right at a marker post and walk up a mossy forest ride.

2 **NN977039** Go through a gate in a high deer fence and turn right, leaving the Reservoirs Trail. A grassy path leads uphill beside the fence and a ruined stone wall. Soon pass an intermediate top and continue up a long ridge to the summit of Innerdownie Hill (610m/2001ft).

3 **NN966051** Continue along the fence line, crossing the slight rise of Bentie Hill then going over a ladder stile in a fence on the north flank of Whitewisp Hill (there is a dog gate beside it). Turn right along the fence, which soon rejoins the stone wall along the ridge. Cross a shallow col and climb steadily up Tarmangie Hill (645m/2116ft), reaching the summit via a gate in the wall. Head back to the wall and go downhill beside it to a crossing point in the deer fence at the head of Glen Sherup.

4 NN937014 Go through and continue diagonally right, following a quad bike track. This climbs on to the side of the broad ridge. Once past Scad Hill, a long descent takes you to the foot of Ben Shee. Pass through an old stone wall then follow the more substantial track that passes over the shoulder of Ben Shee. Follow this gravelly track around the north side of the hill and down the northeast ridge, called The Shank. The track heads towards Glensherup Farm, angling off the ridge to another crossing point in a deer fence.

5 NN962049 Go through and turn right down the fence through sheep pasture. At the bottom, go right along the tarmac road leading to Glensherup Reservoir. Beyond Glensherup

House, go left to cross the bridge over the spillway and walk along the grassy dam. Beyond a gap in a fence, a short, steep scramble takes you up to the forest road. Turn left to return to the car park.

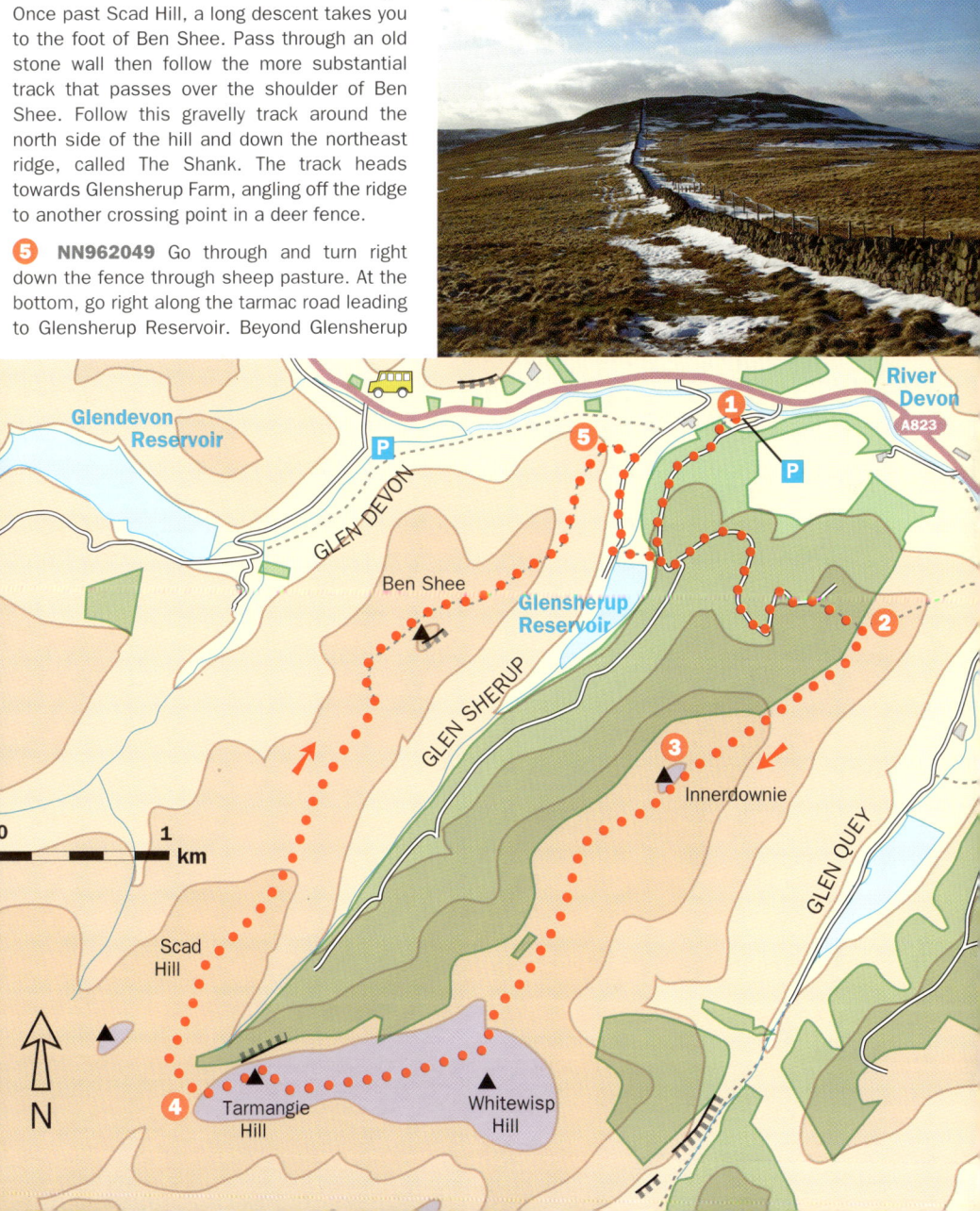

12

Perthshire's highest mountain rises steeply between Loch Tay and lovely Glen Lyon. As well as being a magnificent viewpoint, it is famous for its mountain flowers.

Ben Lawers

Start	Ben Lawers car park **NN608379**
Distance	11.2km (7 miles)
Grade	▢ ▢ ▢ ▢ ▢
Time	5 hours
Terrain	High mountains with steep drops; stony but well maintained paths with many rock steps
Ascent	900m (2950ft)

Getting there: Ben Lawers car park is signed 19km (12 miles) along Loch Tay on the A827 from Kenmore. It is then 3km (2 miles) up a steep, narrow road.

Public transport: Several bus services run along the A827 between Aberfeldy and Killin.

Ben Lawers National Nature Reserve extends over the Ben Lawers range of mountains and the neighbouring Tarmachan range. Ben Lawers is the tenth highest Munro (mountain over 3,000ft) in Scotland. Its limestone-rich rocks and harsh climate make

it the best place in Britain for arctic-alpine flora. Purple saxifrage flowers as soon as the snow melts, while most other species bloom from June to August. For details of ranger led events and to check with the National Trust for Scotland whether the Visitor Centre at the car park is open, you can visit www.nts.org.uk/Property/94/.

Two Munros are climbed on this route, as Ben Lawers is approached over the top of Beinn Ghlas. It begins through a nature trail where an area around the Burn of Edramucky has been fenced against grazing animals and planted with trees. The vegetation within the fence is much more luxuriant than on the open hill. Above the enclosure, the walk is an exposed mountain climb into a colder, windier environment. Make sure that you are appropriately equipped.

1 **NN608379** Leave the car park by a boardwalk that leads across a marshy area towards the Nature Trail. Go through a gate and up the main path. Halfway up, the path swings over the burn and continues uphill on the far side.

2 **NN615392** Exit the enclosure at the top right hand corner by another gate. Climb beyond to a path junction by a large boulder and keep straight on uphill. The good path with some natural rock steps zigzags steeply uphill. The gradient eases for a while as it reaches a ridge and bends left along it – a good place to pause for a breather and to admire the view westwards over Loch Tay. More steep slopes and a final ascent of rock slabs take you to the top of Beinn Ghlas (1103m/3619ft).

3 **NN625404** The summit only has a small cairn, but it is a pronounced peak with a precipitous drop on the north side where ravens often play in the air currents. Follow the path northeast down a steep-sided ridge towards craggy Ben Lawers. Cross the col between the mountains, where there is a tiny lochan on the right, and continue on the steep rocky path up Ben Lawers.

4 **NN635414** A steep haul up eroded rock steps and loose stones brings you to the summit of Ben Lawers (1214m/3983 feet), marked by a round stone pillar and a concrete trig point. A stunning view stretches ahead to other Munros – An Stuc, Meall Garbh and Meall Greigh – that encircle a corrie containing beautiful Lochan nan Cat. Return down the same path to the col.

5 **NN630411** At the col, fork right on a narrow path that trends gently downhill below the steep north face of Beinn Ghlas. The long, wide valley of Allt a' Chobhair runs away on the right to Glen Lyon. Beyond a stream crossing, the path

contours around the north ridge of the mountain. At the marshy col between Beinn Ghlas and Meall Corranaich, cross a line of old metal fence posts and keep straight ahead on a path that angles down the left side of the Burn of Edramucky. Descend gently to the path junction at the large boulder and turn right to return through the fenced enclosure.

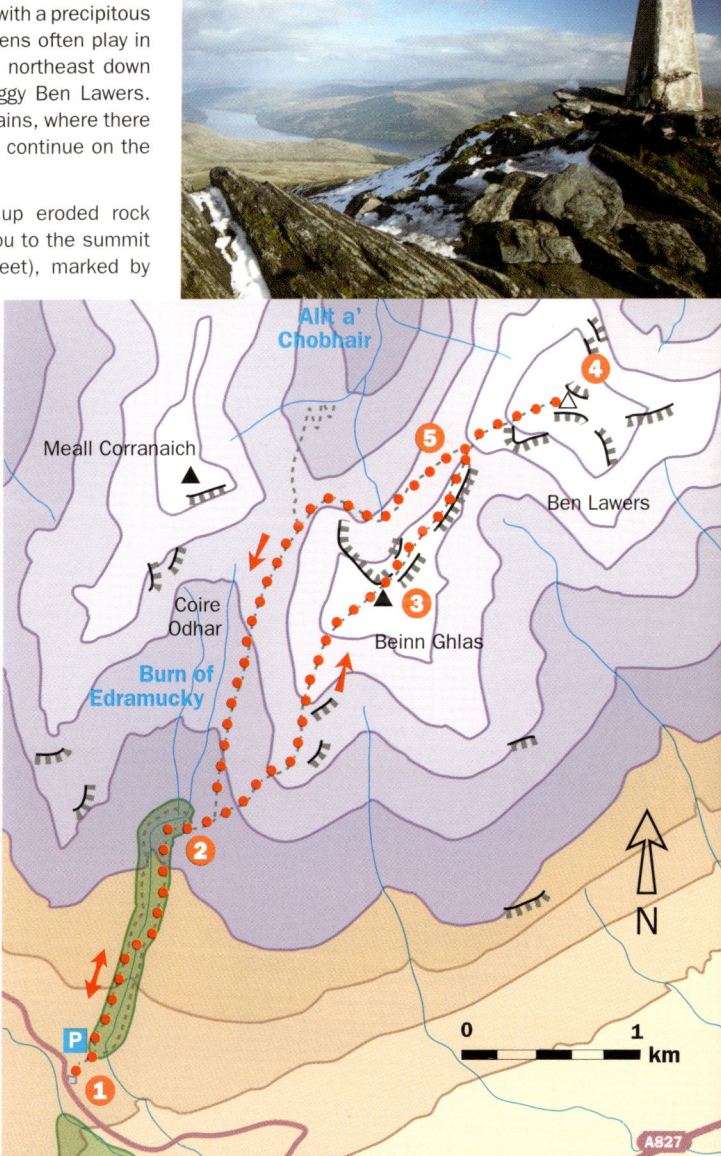

OPPOSITE
Ben Lawers from the Beinn Ghlas path to the col

ABOVE
View east up Loch Tay from the Ben Lawers summit

Enjoying the outdoors

Perth and Kinross Council have a duty to uphold public access rights and you should contact their access officers if you find any route obstructed. The council employs countryside rangers, who help people to enjoy the outdoors responsibly and who organise events such as guided wildlife walks.

Several other organisations also promote access on their land – often with waymarked paths – and employ rangers who assist the public and carry out nature conservation work.

A Perthshire Big Tree Country guide to Countryside Events and Guided Walks is published each year, listing outdoor events being organised by these various organisations. There is also a Perthshire Big Tree Country guide to dozens of places you can visit to enjoy the area's unique woodland heritage and magnificent landscape. These free guides can be picked up at visitor information centres.

Perth and Kinross Council
Community Greeenspace
01738 475349
www.pkc.gov.uk

Forestry Commission Scotland
Tay Forest Park
01350 728641
www.forestry.gov.uk

Scottish Natural Heritage
01738 444177
www.snh.org.uk

The National Trust for Scotland
01350 728641
www.nts.org.uk

Scottish Wildlife Trust
Loch of the Lowes
01350 727337
www.swt.org.uk

Atholl Estates
01796 481646 or 481355
www.athollestatesrangerservice.co.uk

Enjoy Scotland's outdoors responsibly

Everyone has the right to be on most land and inland water providing they act responsibly. Your access rights and responsibilities are explained fully in the Scottish Outdoor Access Code.

Whether you're in the outdoors or managing the outdoors, the key things are to:

- **take responsibility for your own actions**
- **respect the interests of other people**
- **care for the environment.**

Visit **outdooraccess-scotland.com** or contact your local Scottish Natural Heritage office.

SCOTTISH OUTDOOR ACCESS CODE

KNOW THE CODE BEFORE YOU GO
outdooraccess-scotland.com